Especially for

_____

From

_____

Date

_____

Published by Barbour Publishing, Inc., P.O. Box 719, Uhrichsville, Ohio 44683, www.barbourbooks.com

Our mission is to publish and distribute inspirational products offering exceptional value and biblical encouragement to the masses.

 Member of the
Evangelical Christian
Publishers Association

Printed in China.

EXPRESSIONS OF
JOY FOR
Women

BARBOUR
PUBLISHING

Eternal Pleasures

You have made known to me the path of life; you
will fill me with joy in your presence, with eternal
pleasures at your right hand.

PSALM 16:11 NIV

Spiritual Joys

How long has it been since you have allowed
yourself to experience the spiritual joys of life?
Don't let the day's troubles, a busy schedule, or other
distractions strip you of the everyday pleasures God has
set before you. Consider the fact that He has called you
to be His own. Meditate on His presence in your life
and what it means to you. Give thanks today for the
blessings of the day and experience
His love for you!

PATRICIA MITCHELL AND
REBECCA CURRINGTON

Never Give Up

When you get into a tight place and everything goes against you, till it seems as though you cannot hang on a minute longer, never give up then, for that is just the place and time that the tide will turn.

HARRIET BEECHER STOWE

A Real Friend

A real friend is not so much someone you feel free to be serious with as someone you feel free to be silly with.

SYDNEY J. HARRIS

The Happiest People

I think I began learning long ago that those who are the happiest are those who do the most for others.

BOOKER T. WASHINGTON

A Kind Heart

A kind heart is a fountain of gladness, making
everything in its vicinity freshen into smiles.

WASHINGTON IRVING

Overflowing Joy

Want to know the secret of walking in the fullness of joy? Draw near to the Lord. Allow His Spirit to fill you daily. Let Him whisper sweet nothings in your ear and woo you with His love. The Spirit of God is your Comforter, your Friend. He fills you to overflowing. Watch the joy flow!

JANICE HANNA

Joy Will Come

Having trouble finding joy in your life today? Do what
the psalmists often did and remind yourself what
God has already done for you. How many ways has
following Him blessed you? Begin by thanking Him
for His saving grace, and the joy starts, no matter what
you face today. Your lips will show the delight
in your heart.

PAMELA MCQUADE

Spread Happiness

Happiness is like jam. You can't spread even a little without getting some on yourself.

UNKNOWN

Laugh till You Cry!

Every now and then, it's delightful to have the kind of
laughter that makes your stomach jiggle, that sends
tears down your face, and that causes your eyes to
squint so it's impossible to see!

BONNIE JENSEN

Making Your Mark

If the essence of my being has caused a smile to have appeared upon your face or a touch of joy within your heart—then in living—I have made my mark.

THOMAS L. ODEM JR.

Friends Ensure Happiness

Of all the means to ensure happiness throughout
the whole of life, by far the most important is the
acquisition of friends.

EPICURUS

A Vision of Joy

O Lord, share with me the vision to find joy
everywhere: in the wild violet's beauty, in the lark's
melody, in a child's smile, in a mother's love,
in the purity of Jesus.

SCOTS CELTIC PRAYER

Expect the Best

God has promised to give you good things if you obey Him. You may not get the blessing right now, but don't lose heart; God has not forgotten you. Be patient and expect only the best from Him.

PAMELA MCQUADE

Two Requirements for Prayer

There are two requirements for our prayer: enjoyment of every earthly blessing which God bestows on us— a thankful reflection on the goodness of the Giver and a deep sense of the unworthiness of the receiver. The first would make us grateful, the second humble.

HANNAH MORE

Praise God

O God, great and wonderful, who has created the
heavens, dwelling in the light and beauty of it;
who has made the earth, revealing Yourself in every
flower that opens; let not my eyes be blind to You,
neither my heart to be dead, but teach me to praise You,
even as the lark which offers her song at daybreak.

ISIDORE OF SEVILLE

Season of Joy

Want to know how to get beyond a season of
heaviness? Want to enter a season of joy?
Speak uplifting, positive words. The things that come
out of your mouth can make or break you. After all,
we tend to believe what we hear. So, let words of joy
flow. Speak hope. Speak life. And watch that spirit of
heaviness take flight!

JANICE HANNA

The Way to Success

To appreciate beauty; to find the best in others;
to give one's self; to leave the world a little better. . .
to have played and laughed with enthusiasm,
and sung with exultation; to know even one life has
breathed easier because you have lived. . .
This is to have succeeded.

RALPH WALDO EMERSON

Rejoice in All Things

There is not one blade of grass, there is no color in
the world that is not intended to make us rejoice.

JOHN CALVIN

What Matters Most

What matters is not your outer appearance—the styling of your hair, the jewelry you wear, the cut of your clothes—but your inner disposition. Cultivate inner beauty, the gentle, gracious kind that God delights in.

I PETER 3:3–4 MSG

God Gives Us Joy

I asked God for all things, that I might enjoy life.
God gave me life that I might enjoy all things.

UNKNOWN

Whole Heart!

Consider today what you have to be thankful for
and then give thanks with your whole heart.

AMBER JAMES

Don't Miss the Little Things

Don't ever let yourself get so busy that you miss those little but important extras in life—the beauty of a day. . .the smile of a friend. . .the serenity of a quiet moment alone. For it is often life's smallest pleasures and gentlest joys that make the biggest and most lasting difference.

UNKNOWN

The Golden Circle

If you truly love and enjoy your friends, they are part of the golden circle that makes life good.

MARJORIE HOLMES

Praise God—
No Matter What

Need some joy in your life? Start praising God, and no matter what messy situations you face today, you'll begin rejoicing. Praise Him for who He is—His immense, loving nature that has blessed you so much. Thank Him for the love He's showered on you. As you remember His love, sorrow loses its grasp on your life.

PAMELA MCQUADE

God Created Us for Himself

God's great purpose for the human race [is] that He created us for Himself. This realization of our election by God is the most joyful on earth, and we must learn to rely on this tremendous creative purpose of God.

OSWALD CHAMBERS

Extraordinary Blessing

Don't you enjoy walking through seasons of
extraordinary blessing? We can hardly believe it when
God's "more than enough" provision shines down
upon us. What did we do to deserve it? Nothing!
During such seasons, we can't forget to thank Him
for the many ways He is moving in our lives.
Our hearts must overflow with gratitude to a gracious
and almighty God.

JANICE HANNA

Let Nothing Escape You

Half the joy of life is in little things taken on the run.
Let us run if we must—even the sands do that—
but let us keep our hearts young and our eyes open
that nothing worth our while shall escape us.
And everything is worth its while if we only grasp it
and its significance.

C. VICTOR CHERBULIEZ

Be "Heavenly Hip!"

The Lord is there through thick and thin. . . . Let Him be the stability in your life. Run to God when you feel overwhelmed by the changes going on around you. If you'll stay grounded in Him, you'll always be "heavenly hip" and ready to face anything!

MICHELLE MEDLOCK ADAMS

Humor Is a Great Thing

Humor is the great thing, the saving thing.
The minute it crops up, all our irritation and resentments
slip away, and a sunny spirit takes their place.

MARK TWAIN

God Knows All About Us

[God] knows everything about us. And He cares about everything. Moreover, He can manage every situation. And He loves us! Surely this is enough to open the wellsprings of joy. . . . And joy is always a source of strength.

HANNAH WHITALL SMITH

The Best Feelings

There are no better feelings in life than the feelings you experience when you are surrounded by the friends you love.

UNKNOWN

The Shortest Way to Happiness

If anyone would tell you the shortest, surest way
to happiness and all perfection, he must tell you to
make it a rule to yourself to thank and praise God for
everything that happens to you. For it is certain that
whatever seeming calamity happens to you, if you
thank and praise God for it, you turn it into a blessing.

WILLIAM LAW

Revel in the Joy

If your heart is full from the blessings God has rained on you lately, revel in this season of joy and let your laughter reverberate to the heavens.

UNKNOWN

Humor Smoothes the Rough Spots

Humor makes our heavy burdens light and smoothes the rough spots in our pathways.

SAM ERVIN

Greet Each Day with Joy

If the day and the night are such that you greet them with joy, and life emits a fragrance like flowers and sweet-scented herbs, is more elastic, more starry, more immortal—that is your success.

HENRY DAVID THOREAU

Sharing Joy

Joy is meant to be shared. (It's hard to keep to yourself, after all!) Think of it like a tasty apple pie. You can't eat the whole thing, can you? No, you need to spread the love, share the slices. So it is with joy. When you're going through a particularly joyful season, pass the plates. Sharing is half the fun!

JANICE HANNA

Catch the Trade Winds

Twenty years from now you will be more
disappointed by the things you didn't do than by
the ones you did do. So throw off the bowlines.
Sail away from the safe harbor. Catch the trade
winds in your sails. Explore. Dream. Discover.

MARK TWAIN

Our Souls Blossom

Let us be grateful to people who make us happy;
they are the charming gardeners who make our
souls blossom.

MARCEL PROUST

DAY 40

God's Best

"If God gives such attention to the appearance of wildflowers—most of which are never ever seen—don't you think he'll attend to you, take pride in you, do his best for you?"

MATTHEW 6:30 MSG

Immerse Yourself in God's Presence

The old saying might ring true for you right now:
"Laugh and the world laughs with you; cry and you
cry alone." Yet you know you're not alone when you
weep. God remains at your side with the comfort of
His peace, relief, and yes, laughter. Seem impossible?
Not with God. Not when you immerse yourself in His
presence today and bathe in the certainty of a better
tomorrow. Let Him fill your life with laughter!

PATRICIA MITCHELL
AND REBECCA CURRINGTON

Extreme Makeover

Let Jesus and His light fill you up and flow out of
you. Continue to look into the Word and allow
His light to reveal areas where you need growth.
As you do this, you'll find that you are being
transformed from Bozo to Beauty.
Talk about an extreme makeover!

MICHELLE
MEDLOCK ADAMS

The Light Within

People are like stained glass windows; they sparkle and shine when the sun is out, but when the darkness sets in their true beauty is revealed only if there is a light within.

ELISABETH KÜBLER-ROSS

The Footpath to Peace

Be glad of life, because it gives you the chance to love
and to work and to play and to look up at the stars. . .
and to spend as much time as you can, with body and
with spirit, in God's out-of-doors—these are little
guideposts on the footpath to peace.

HENRY VAN DYKE

Jesus Never Changes

Do we live as if God really means what He says?
When we read scripture, do we believe He will
provide all He promises? Can we trust that as His
Spirit calls our hearts to action, He will empower us
to complete the task? Jesus kept all His first-century
promises, and He hasn't changed in twenty centuries.
He'll keep His word to us, too.

PAMELA MCQUADE

Don't Wait

Do not keep the alabaster boxes of your kindness
sealed up until your friends are gone.
Speak approving, cheering words while their ears
can hear them—and be happier by them.

GEORGE WILLIAM CHILDS

God Loves You Today and Always

You are loved. . .incredibly, sacrificially loved by the King of kings. Doesn't that fill you with overwhelming joy? Can you sense His heart for you? God's love is not based on anything you have done or will ever do. No. That amazing love was poured out on Calvary and beckons us daily. You are loved—today and always.

JANICE HANNA

Know You Are Precious

If we know Jesus Christ and have responded to His invitation to receive Him as Savior, Jesus remains forever our advocate before the Father, saying with love, "She's mine." Know that you are so precious to Jesus that He gave His life for you. Doesn't it feel incredible to have Jesus as your defender?

CAROL L. FITZPATRICK

Ignore the Inconsequential

Do not let trifles disturb your tranquility of mind. . . .
Life is too precious to be sacrificed for the nonessential
and transient. . . . Ignore the inconsequential.

GRENVILLE KLEISER

Friendships Hold Blessings

God's goodness to us is revealed in our
friendships. They hold the blessings we were
created to enjoy but can't possibly number—
laughter, encouragement, compassion,
generosity, forgiveness, and love.

BONNIE JENSEN

A Sunbeam

Happiness is a sunbeam. . . . When it strikes a kindred
heart, like the converged lights upon a mirror,
it reflects itself with redoubled brightness. It is not
perfected until it is shared.

JANE PORTER

A Good Laugh Bursts from the Soul

A smile starts on the lips, a grin spreads to the eyes, a chuckle comes from the belly; but a good laugh bursts forth from the soul, overflows, and bubbles all around.

CAROLYN BIRMINGHAM

Never Lose an Opportunity

Never lose an opportunity of seeing anything that is beautiful; for beauty is God's handwriting—a wayside sacrament. Welcome it in every fair face, in every fair sky, in every fair flower, and thank God for it as a cup of blessing.

RALPH WALDO EMERSON

An Irish Blessing

May there always be work for your hands to do.
May your purse always hold a coin or two.
May the sun always shine on your windowpane.
May a rainbow be certain to follow each rain.

IRISH BLESSING

The Wonder of the World

I still find each day too short for all the thoughts I want to think, all the walks I want to take, all the books I want to read, and all the friends I want to see. The longer I live, the more my mind dwells upon the beauty and the wonder of the world.

JOHN BURROUGHS

Friends Make Us Grow

Close friends contribute to our personal growth.
They also contribute to our personal pleasure,
making the music sound sweeter, the wine taste richer,
the laughter ring louder because they are there.

JUDITH VIORST

Joyful in Love

When you love the Lord and recognize His great love for you, it's easy to be joyful! Think of His marvelous deeds. Relish His overwhelming love for His children. Recognize His daily blessings. Oh, may we never forget that the Lord our God longs for us to see the depth of His love for us. . .and to love Him fully in return.

JANICE HANNA

Footprints

Friendship is like standing in wet cement.
The longer you stay, the harder it is to leave,
and you can never go without leaving your
footprints behind.

UNKNOWN

Supreme Happiness

The supreme happiness of life is the conviction that
we are loved—loved for ourselves, or rather, in spite of
ourselves.

VICTOR HUGO

God Takes Care of Everything

You can be sure that God will take care of everything you need, his generosity exceeding even yours in the glory that pours from Jesus. Our God and Father abounds in glory that just pours out into eternity.

PHILIPPIANS 4:19–20 MSG

Celebrate!

Celebrate the happiness that friends are always giving;
make every day a holiday and celebrate just living!

AMANDA BRADLEY

The Root of All Things

The wonder of living is held within the beauty
of silence, the glory of sunlight, the sweetness of
fresh spring air, the quiet strength of earth,
and the love that lies at the very root of all things.

UNKNOWN

A Journey Set in Motion

There is something satisfying, rejuvenating, comforting about the seasons. They remind me that I play one small part in a much bigger picture—that there is a pulse, a sequence, a journey set into motion by the very hand of God Himself.

KAREN SCALF LINAMEN

The Living Expression

Be the living expression of God's kindness; kindness is your face, kindness in your eyes, kindness in your smile.

MOTHER TERESA

Rest

Rest is not idleness, and to lie sometimes on the grass under the trees on a summer's day, listening to the murmur of the water or watching the clouds float across the sky, is by no means a waste of time.

SIR JOHN LUBBOCK

Sense of the Beautiful

A person should hear a little music, read a little poetry, and see a fine picture every day of their life, in order that worldly cares may not obliterate the sense of the beautiful which God has implanted in the human soul.

JOHANN WOLFGANG VON GOETHE

Everyday Joy

Every breath we breathe comes from God. Every step
we take is a gift from our Creator. We can do nothing
apart from Him. In the same sense, every joy, every
sorrow. . .God goes through each one with us.
His heart is for us. We can experience joy in our
everyday lives, even when things aren't going our way.
We simply have to remember that He is in control.
We have our being. . .in Him!

JANICE HANNA

Laughing Together

When people are laughing together, there are no age differences, no racial barriers, and no economic distinctions. It is just people enjoying their existence.

BRUCE BICKEL AND STAN JANTZ

Warm Memories and Shared Joys

Friendship is like a Christmas tree, decorated with warm memories and shared joys.

UNKNOWN

Keep Love in Your Heart

Keep love in your heart. A life without it is like
a sunless garden when the flowers are dead.
The consciousness of loving and being loved
brings a warmth and richness to life that
nothing else can bring.

OSCAR WILDE

Prayer Unites the Soul with God

Prayer is an upward leap of the heart, an untroubled glance toward heaven, a cry of gratitude and love which I utter from the depths of sorrow as well as from the heights of joy. It has supernatural grandeur that expands the soul and unites it with God.

THÉRÈSE OF LISIEUX

A New Life

A new life begins for us with every second. Let us go forward joyously to meet it. We must press on, whether we will or no, and we shall walk better with our eyes before us than with them ever cast behind.

JEROME K. JEROME

Rekindle the Inner Spirit

In everyone's life, at some time, our inner fire goes out. It is then burst into flame by an encounter with another human being. We should all be thankful for those people who rekindle the inner spirit.

ALBERT SCHWEITZER

Be a Friend

The most I can do for my friend is simply to be
his friend. I have no wealth to bestow on him.
If he knows that I am happy in loving him,
he will want no other reward.

HENRY DAVID THOREAU

The Joy of Living

Whether sixty or sixteen, there is in every human being's heart the love of wonder, the sweet amazement at the stars and starlike things, the undaunted challenge of events, the unfailing childlike appetite for what-next, and the joy of the game of living.

SAMUEL ULLMAN

Instrument of Peace

Lord, make me an instrument of Your peace.
Where there is hatred, let me bring love. Where
there is offense, forgiveness. Where there is discord,
reconcilation. Where there is doubt, faith.
Where there is despair, hope. Where there is sadness,
joy. Where there is darkness, Your light.

FRANCIS OF ASSISI

Gratitude

Gratitude consists in a watchful, minute attention
to the particulars of our state, and to the multitude
of God's gifts, taken one by one. It fills us with a
consciousness that God loves and cares for us, even to
the least event and smallest need in life.

HENRY EDWARD MANNING

He Loves You!

God does not give His love in dribs and drabs.
He lavishes it on us when we come to Him in
faith. All along, He was waiting to make us His
children, and we were the ones who resisted.
But once we face Him as children, God's love lets
loose in our lives. Nothing is too good for His
obedient children. Praise God that
He loves you that much!

PAMELA MCQUADE

The Joy of His Presence

When God finds a soul that rests in Him and is not easily moved, He operates within it in His own manner. . . . He gives to such a soul the key to the treasures He has prepared for it so that it might enjoy them. And to this same soul He gives the joy of His presence which entirely absorbs such a soul.

CATHERINE OF GENOA

Filled with Joy

And the disciples were filled with joy, and with the
Holy Ghost.

ACTS 13:52 KJV

Humor Is a Natural Resource

Humor is a serious thing. I like to think of it as one of our greatest, earliest natural resources, which must be preserved at all cost.

JAMES THURBER

Free and Unrestricted

One who loves is borne on wings; he runs,
and is filled with joy; he is free and unrestricted.
He gives all to receive all, and he has all in all;
for beyond all things he rests in the one highest
thing, from whom streams all that is good.

THOMAS À KEMPIS

Little Drops of Water

Little drops of water,
Little grains of sand,
Make the mighty ocean
And the beauteous land.
Little deeds of kindness,
Little words of love,
Make our earth an Eden,
Like the Heaven above.

JULIA FLETCHER CARNEY

Abundant Joy

Huge waves that would frighten an ordinary swimmer produce a tremendous thrill for the surfer who has ridden them. Let's apply that to our own circumstances. The things we try to avoid and fight against—tribulation, suffering, and persecution— are the very things that produce abundant joy in us.

OSWALD CHAMBERS

Thy Will Be Done

My Jesus, as Thou wilt!
O may Thy will be mine!
Into Thy hand of love
I would my all resign
Through sorrow or through joy,
Conduct me as Thine own;
And help me still to say,
My Lord, Thy will be done.

BENJAMIN SCHMOLK

A Life of Joy

Want to know the perfect recipe for happiness?
Spend your days focused on making others
happy. If you shift your focus from yourself to
others, you accomplish two things: You put
others first, and you're always looking for ways
to make others smile. There's something about
spreading joy that satisfies the soul.

JANICE HANNA

Richly Blessed

I asked for riches that I might be wise. I asked for power that I might feel the need of God. I asked for all things that I might enjoy all things. I got nothing that I asked for, but everything that I had hoped for. Almost despite myself, my unspoken prayers were answered; I am, among all men, most richly blessed.

UNKNOWN CONFEDERATE SOLDIER

The Joy of a Friend

Words cannot express the joy which a friend imparts; they only can know who have experienced. A friend is dearer than the light of heaven, for it would be better for us that the sun were to extinguish than we should be without friends.

JOHN CHRYSOSTOM

Through the Power

To live content with small means. . .
To study hard, think quietly, talk gently, act frankly;
To listen to stars and birds, to babes and sages,
    with open hearts;
To bear all cheerfully, do all bravely, await occasions,
    hurry never.
In a word, to let the spiritual,
    unbidden and unconscious,
Grow up through the common.

WILLIAM HENRY CHANNING

The Lord's Chief Desire

The Lord's chief desire is to reveal Himself to you and, in order for Him to do that, He gives you the experience of enjoying His presence. He touches you, and His touch is so delightful that, more than ever, you are drawn inwardly to Him.

MADAME JEANNE GUYON

Simple Charm

The splendor of the rose and the whiteness of the lily do not rob the little violet of its scent nor the daisy of its simple charm. If every tiny flower wanted to be a rose, Spring would lose its loveliness.

THÉRÈSE OF LISIEUX

Complete Joy

The God of the universe—the One who created everything and holds it all in His hands—created each of us in His image, to bear His likeness, His imprint. It is only when Christ dwells within our hearts, radiating the pure light of His love through our humanity, that we discover who we are and what we

were intended to be. There is no other joy that reaches as deep or as wide or as high—there is no other joy that is more complete.

JOANIE GARBORG

Let Us Dwell with the Lord

Bring us, O Lord God. . .to enter into that gate and
dwell in that house, where there shall be no darkness
nor dazzling, but one equal light; no noise nor silence,
but one equal music. . .no ends nor beginnings,
but one equal eternity; in the habitations of Your
majesty and Your glory, world without end.

JOHN DONNE

Life Is Good

Oh, the wild joys of living!
The leaping from rock up to rock. . .
How good is. . .life, the mere living!
How fit to employ
All the heart and the soul
And the senses forever in joy!

ROBERT BROWNING

The Joys of Friendship

We don't need soft skies to make friendship a joy to us.
What a heavenly thing it is; world without end, truly.
I grow warm thinking of it, and should glow at the
thought if all the glaciers of the Alps were heaped over
me! Such friends God has given me in this little life of
mine!

CELIA LAIGHTON THAXTER

The Real Joy of Life

The real joy of life is in its play. Play is anything we do
for the joy and love of doing it, apart from any profit,
compulsion, or sense of duty. It is the real living of life
with the feeling of freedom and self-expression. Play is
the business of childhood, and its continuation in later
years is the prolongation of youth.

WALTER RAUSCHENBUSCH

He Gently Leads Us

God gives us everything we need to make it through life. He teaches us His ways. Fills us with His joy. Gives us the pleasure of meeting with Him for times of intimate worship. What an awesome teacher and friend. He takes us by the hand and gently leads us. . . from experience to experience. . .joy to joy.

JANICE HANNA

Children of God

Peace of conscience, liberty of heart,
the sweetness of abandoning ourselves in the
hands of God, the joy of always seeing the light
grow in our hearts, finally, freedom from the
fears and insatiable desires of the times, multiply
a hundredfold the happiness which the true
children of God possess.

FRANÇOIS FÉNELON

Spread the Joy

Tell this news with shouts of joy to the people;
spread it everywhere on earth.

ISAIAH 48:20 NCV

Enjoy the Journey

In such a beautiful wilderness of wildflowers, we are
amused with the variety and novelty of the scene
so much that we in our pleasure lose all sense of
weariness or fatigue in the length of our wanderings
and get to the end before we are aware of our journey.

JOHN CLARE

Heaven Breaking Through

All that is sweet, delightful, and amiable in this world,
in the serenity of the air, the fineness of seasons,
the joy of light, the melody of sounds, the beauty
of colors, the fragrance of smells, the splendor of
precious stones, is nothing else but Heaven breaking
through the veil of this world.

SIR FRANCIS BACON

Memories

Sometimes our thoughts turn back toward
a corner in a forest, or the end of a bank, or
an orchard powered with flowers, seen but a
single time. . .yet remaining in our hearts and
leaving in soul and body an unappeased desire
which is not to be forgotten, a feeling we have
just rubbed elbows with happiness.

GUY DE MAUPASSANT

Renewed

By reading the scriptures I am so renewed that all nature seems renewed around me and with me. The sky seems to be a pure, a cooler blue, the trees a deeper green. The whole world is charged with the glory of God, and I feel fire and music under my feet.

THOMAS MERTON

Lightly!

Angels fly because they take themselves lightly.

UNKNOWN

Friends Make Life More Fun

I cannot imagine where I would be today were it not for that handful of friends who have given me a heart full of joy. Let's face it, friends make life a lot more fun.

CHARLES SWINDOLL

Exercise

The greatest exercise for strengthening the heart
is reaching down and lifting people up.

ERNEST BLEVINS

An Expansion of One's Self

There is one friend in the life of each of us who seems not a separate person, however dear and beloved, but an expansion, an interpretation, of one's self, the very meaning of one's soul.

EDITH WHARTON

Small Pleasures

Happiness consists more in small conveniences or pleasures that occur every day, than in great pieces of good fortune that happen but seldom to a man in the course of his life.

BENJAMIN FRANKLIN

Have Faith

Never forget that you are not alone. God is with you,
helping and guiding. He is the companion who never
fails, the friend whose love comforts and strengthens.
Have faith, and He will do everything for you.

AUROBINDO

A Hopeful Impulse

Every heart that has beat strong and cheerfully
has left a hopeful impulse behind it in the world
and bettered the tradition of mankind.

ROBERT LOUIS STEVENSON

Soar!

We look at our burdens and heavy loads and
shrink from them; but as we lift them and bind
them about our hearts, they become wings,
and on them we rise and soar toward God.

MRS. CHARLES COWMAN

God Is Everywhere

There's not a tint that paints the rose
Or decks the lily fair,
Or marks the humblest flower that grows,
But God has placed it there. . . .
There's not a place on earth's vast round,
        In oceans deep or air,
        Where love and beauty are not found,
        For God is everywhere.

JAMES C. WALLACE

Nature's Joyous Song

All of nature sings the praises of our mighty God. Look around you! Do you see the hills off in the distance, pointing up in majesty? Can you hear the water in the brooks, tumbling along in a chorus of praise? And what about the ocean waves? Oh, the joy in discovering the God of the universe through His marvelous creation!

JANICE HANNA

Element of Joy

Into many lives, in many simple, familiar, homely ways, God infuses this element of joy from the surprises of life, which unexpectedly brighten our days and fill our eyes with light.

HENRY WADSWORTH LONGFELLOW

Instruments of God

The art of life is to live in the present moment
and to make that moment as perfect as we can by
the realization that we are the instruments and
expression of God Himself.

EMMET FOX

The Best Things in Life

The best things in life are nearest: breath in your
nostrils, light in your eyes, flowers at your feet,
duties at your hand, the path of God just before you.

ROBERT LOUIS STEVENSON

Tomorrow. . .

Embrace the wonder and excitement each day brings.
For tomorrow affords us new opportunities. . .
time to experience. . .time to create. . .time to reflect. . .
time to dream.

K. WILLIAMS

Eternal Hope

Life is what we are alive to. It is not length
but breadth. . . . Be alive to. . .goodness,
kindness, purity, love, history, poetry, music,
flowers, stars, God, and eternal hope.

MALTBIE D. BABCOCK

Songs of Joy

Our mouths were filled with laughter, our tongues
with songs of joy.

PSALM 126:2 NIV

As the Month of May

Let all thy joys be as the month of May,
And all thy days be as a marriage day:
Let sorrow, sickness, and a troubled mind
Be a stranger to thee.

FRANCIS QUARLES

The Greatest Blessing

The lives that have been the greatest blessing to you
are the lives of those people who themselves were
unaware of having been a blessing.

OSWALD CHAMBERS

Love Is a Great Gift

Love is a great thing, an altogether good gift;
the only thing that makes burdens light and
bears all that is hard with ease. It carries a weight
without feeling it and makes all that is bitter
sweet and pleasant to the taste.

THOMAS À KEMPIS

Sense of Humor

The sense of humor is the oil of life's engine.
Without it, the machinery creaks and groans.
No lot is so hard, no aspect of things is so grim,
but it relaxes before a hearty laugh.

GEORGE S. MERRIAM

Laughter Is Sunshine

A good laugh is sunshine in the house.

WILLIAM MAKEPEACE THACKERAY

God Equips Us

Each of us may be sure that if God sends us on stony paths, He will provide us with strong shoes, and He will not send us out on any journey for which He does not equip us well.

ALEXANDER MACLAREN

Never Lose Sight

We may run, walk, stumble. . .or fly, but let us never lose sight of the reason for the journey or miss a chance to see a rainbow on the way.

GLORIA GAITHER

Delight in Him

Even when fear or stress challenges you, you need to
deal with it single-handedly, if Jesus rules your life.
When your life seems in shambles around you,
He offers strength and comfort for a hurting heart.
God never gives up on you. His love cannot change.
Today, delight in the One who never deserts you.

PAMELA MCQUADE

Hints of What Shall Be

Human love and the delights of friendship, out of
which are built the memories that endure, are also to
be treasured up as hints of what shall be hereafter.

BEDE JARRETT

True Happiness

True happiness comes when we stop complaining about all the troubles we have and offer thanks for all the troubles we don't have.

UNKNOWN

Joy in Small Things

Is it so small a thing to have enjoyed the sun,
to have lived light in the spring, to have loved,
to have thought, to have done?
To have advanced true friends?

MATTHEW ARNOLD

The Simple Things

When we take time to notice the simple things in life, we never lack for encouragement. We discover we are surrounded by limitless hope that's just wearing everyday clothes.

UNKNOWN

God's Riches

May the God of love and peace set your heart at rest and speed you on your journey. May He meanwhile shelter you. . .in the security of trust and in the restful enjoyment of His riches.

RAYMOND OF PENYAFORT

Praise His Holy Name

Sweet hymns of joy in grateful chorus raise we.
Let all within us praise His holy name.
Christ is the Lord, O praise His name forever.
His pow'r and glory ever more proclaim.

JOHN SULLIVAN DWIGHT

Daily Joys

Daily duties are daily joys, because they
are something which God gives us to offer
unto Him, to do our very best,
in acknowledgement of His love.

EDWARD BOUVERIE PUSEY

The Light

And I have felt a presence that disturbs me with the joy of elevated thoughts; a sense sublime of something far more deeply interfused, whose dwelling is the light of setting suns.

WILLIAM WORDSWORTH

God's Love

The Breadth of His Love: "God so loved the world."
The Length: "that He gave His only begotten Son."
The Depth: "that whosoever believeth on Him shall
   not perish."
The Height: "but shall have everlasting life."

UNKNOWN

Within Me

No great works and wonders God has ever wrought or shall ever do in or through His created world, not even God Himself in His goodness will make me blessed if they remain outside of me. For blessedness is only present to the extent to which it is within me.

THEOLOGIA GERMANICA

Things Not Seen

Of all the classes and descriptions of persons on
this earth, they are the happiest of whom it
may be said that the things most hoped
for by them are the things not seen.

MENNONITE WRITINGS

Joyful Together

Let the floods clap their hands: let the hills be
joyful together.

PSALM 98:8 KJV

Quite Happy

How could I be anything but quite happy if I believed always that all the past is forgiven, and all the present furnished with power, and all the future bright with hope.

JAMES SMETHAM

God's Gift

The friend given to you by circumstances over which
you have no control was God's own gift.

FREDERICK ROBERTSON

Fullness of Joy

Our God is so wonderfully good and lovely
and blessed in every way that the mere fact of
belonging to Him is enough for an untellable
fullness of joy!

HANNAH WHITALL SMITH

Filled with Laughter

Memories filled with laughter are the ones we tend to recall over and over again. They hold the unique ability to be just as much fun (sometimes even more!) on the "replay."

BONNIE JENSEN

Enjoy Each Day

Unless each day can be looked back upon by an
individual as one in which she has had some fun,
some joy, some real satisfaction, that day is a loss.

UNKNOWN

Be Healthy. . .Laugh!

People who laugh actually live longer than those who
don't laugh. Few persons realize that health actually
varies according to the amount of laughter.

JAMES J. WALSH

Pleasing God

Everyone wants to be happy, right? We know that our obedience to the Lord results in a life of great joy. But our obedience does something else, too. It brings pleasure to our heavenly Father. When we live uprightly, God is pleased. Today, instead of focusing on your own happiness, give some thought to putting a smile on His face.

JANICE HANNA

A Union of Love

We can share with each other without being threatened by each other's differences because we know that we are united by Christ, and this union is a union of love.

MADELEINE L'ENGLE

God Can See the Future

Every experience God gives us, every person He puts into our lives is the perfect preparation for the future that only He can see.

CORRIE TEN BOOM

Two Ways to Live

There are two ways to live your life. One is as though nothing is a miracle. The other is as though everything is a miracle.

ALBERT EINSTEIN

The Happiness of Life

The happiness of life is made up of minute
fractions—the little soon-forgotten charities
of a kiss or a smile, a kind look,
or heartfelt compliment.

SAMUEL TAYLOR COLERIDGE

Plunge Boldly

Plunge boldly into the thick of life, and seize it
where you will; it is always interesting.

JOHANN WOLFGANG VON GOETHE

DAY 152

Joy and Delight

We have a Father in heaven who is almighty, who loves
His children as He loves His only begotten Son,
and whose very joy and delight it is to. . .help them at
all times and under all circumstances.

GEORGE MUELLER

Happiness Benefits the World

There is no duty we so underrate as the duty of being happy. By being happy, we sow benefits upon the world.

ROBERT LOUIS STEVENSON

Hope and Peace

We light a thousand candles bright
Around the earth today,
And all the beams will shine
Across the heaven's grand display.
Dear brightest star o'er Bethlehem,
O let your precious light
Shine in with hope and peace toward
Men in every home tonight.

SWEDISH CAROL

Joyful Simplicities

Year by year the complexities of this spinning world grow more bewildering, and so each year we need all the more to seek peace and comfort in the joyful simplicities.

UNKNOWN

Endless Wonders

As we grow in our capacities to see and enjoy the delights that God has placed in our lives, life becomes a glorious experience of discovering His endless wonders.

UNKNOWN

Limitless Joy

Did you realize that joy is limitless? It knows no boundaries. Jesus poured Himself out on the cross at Calvary—giving everything—so that you could experience fullness of joy. Even now, God longs to make Himself known to you in such a new and unique way. May you burst at the seams with this limitless joy as you enter His presence today.

JANICE HANNA

Something Wonderful about Laughter

There's something wonderful about making our girlfriends laugh. Maybe it's the sound we love to hear—or the joy we feel in brightening their world for just a moment.

BONNIE JENSEN

A Variety of Gifts

God has given each of you a gift from his great variety of spiritual gifts. Use them well to serve one another.

1 PETER 4:10 NLT

Box of Praise

I wish I had a box, the biggest I could find; I'd fill it right up to the brim with everything that's kind. A box without a lock, of course, and never any key; for everything inside that box would then be offered free. Grateful words for joys received I'd freely give away. Oh, let us open wide a box of praise for every day.

UNKNOWN

Come Let Us Adore Him

Sing, choirs of angels, Sing in exultation!
O sing, all ye citizens of heav'n above;
Glory to God, glory in the highest.
O come, let us adore Him,
O come, let us adore Him,
O come, let us adore Him, Christ the Lord.

JOHN FRANCIS WADE

Take a Stand

It's hard to have a vision for tomorrow if
you're not excited about today! Each day
is a gift, after all, and an opportunity to live
for Christ. Today, take a stand for the things
you believe in. Lift high His name.
Not only will you bring joy to His heart
(and your own), you will find yourself
looking forward to a joy-filled tomorrow.

JANICE HANNA

A Personal Design and Plan

This is the real gift: we have been given the breath of life, designed with a unique, one-of-a-kind soul that exists forever—whether we live it as a joy or with indifference doesn't change the fact that we've been given the gift of being now and forever. Priceless in value, we are handcrafted by God, who has a personal design and plan for each of us.

UNKNOWN

Radiant Joy

Our hearts were made for joy. Our hearts were made
to enjoy the One who created them. Too deeply
planted to be much affected by the ups and downs of
life, this joy is a knowing and a being known by our
Creator. He sets our hearts alight with radiant joy.

UNKNOWN

A Contented Heart

The heart is rich when it is content, and it is always content when its desires are fixed on God. Nothing can bring greater happiness than doing God's will for the love of God.

MIGUEL FEBRES CORDERO-MUÑOZ

Joy Abides Forever

Lord Jesus, I take refuge in You:
At the sight of Your face all my doubts flee away:
Before I have spoken my sorrow, You know it:
Wondrous things You have done,
that I cannot forget:
My sorrow You have banished,
joy abides forever:
Joyful praise to Your name.

UNKNOWN

Love Makes Joys More Intense

Love makes burdens lighter, because you divide them.
It makes joys more intense, because you share them.
It makes you stronger, so that you can reach out and
become involved with life in ways you dared not risk
alone.

UNKNOWN

Alleluia!

Soar we now where Christ has led; Alleluia!
Following our exalted Head; Alleluia!
Made like Him, like Him we rise; Alleluia!
Ours the cross, the grave, the skies. Alleluia!

CHARLES WESLEY

Live Your Life

When you were born, you cried and the world rejoiced. Live your life in such a manner that when you die, the world cries and you rejoice.

INDIAN PROVERB

Never Put Off Until Tomorrow

Never put off until tomorrow what you can do today; because if you enjoy it today, you can do it again tomorrow.

UNKNOWN

Light Is Sown for Us

However things may appear to be, of all possible circumstances, those circumstances in whose midst I am set, these are the best that He could choose for me. We do not know how this is true—where would faith be if we did?—but we do know that all things that happen are full of shining seed. Light is sown for us, not darkness.

UNKNOWN

Harmony

If there is righteousness in the heart, there will be beauty in the character. If there is beauty in the character, if there is harmony in the home, there will be order in the nation. When there is order in the nation, there will be peace in the world.

UNKNOWN

Solid Friendships

I do not wish to treat friendships daintily, but with the roughest courage. When they are real, they are not glass threads or frost-work, but the solidest things we know.

RALPH WALDO EMERSON

Bubbling Joy

Can you feel it. . .that bubbling in your midsection? Can you sense it rising to the surface? Joy comes from the deepest place inside of us, so deep that we often forget it's there at all. Wonder of wonders! It rises up, up, up to the surface and the most delightful thing happens. Troubles vanish. Sorrows disappear. Godly joy has the power to squelch negative emotions. So, let the bubbling begin!

JANICE HANNA

Soul Healing

Your body cannot heal without play. Your mind cannot heal without laughter. Your soul cannot heal without joy.

CATHERINE FENWICK

Surrounded by Friends

There are no better feelings in life than the feelings you experience when you are surrounded by the friends you love.

UNKNOWN

To Be Truly Happy

To be truly happy is a question of how we begin and not of how we end, of what we want and not of what we have.

ROBERT LOUIS STEVENSON

The Sweetest Joy

Friendship is one of the sweetest joys of life.
Many might have failed beneath the bitterness of
their trial had they not found a friend.

CHARLES H. SPURGEON

A Joyful Stand

May he give you the desire of your heart and make all your plans succeed. We will shout for joy when you are victorious and will lift up our banners in the name of our God.

PSALM 20:4–5 NIV

Kindred Spirits

The gift of friendship, both given and received, is joy, love, and nurturing for the heart. The realization that you have met a soul mate, a kindred spirit, is one of life's sweetest gifts!

UNKNOWN

God Is Good

The joyful birds prolong the strain,
Their song with every spring renewed;
The air we breathe, and falling rain,
Each softly whispers: God is good.

JOHN HAMPDEN GURNEY

Count Your Many Blessings

When we start to count flowers,
we cease to count weeds;
When we start to count blessings,
we cease to count needs;
When we start to count laughter,
we cease to count tears;
When we start to count memories,
we cease to count years.

UNKNOWN

Spring

The Spring comes in with all her hues and smells,
In freshness breathing over hills and dells:
O'er woods where May
  her gorgeous drapery flings,
And meads washed fragrant
  by their laughing springs.

JOHN CLARE

No Higher Bliss

Only to sit and think of God,
Oh, what a joy it is!
To think the thought,
To breathe the Name:
Earth has no higher bliss.

FREDERICK W. FABER

Our Highest Happiness

To love God, to serve Him because we love Him, is. . .
our highest happiness. . . . Love makes our labor light.
We serve with enthusiasm where we love with sincerity.

HANNAH MORE

Full of Laughter

Sense of humor; God's great gift causes spirits to uplift, helps to make our bodies mend; lightens burdens; cheers a friend; tickles children; elders grin at this warmth that glows within; surely in the great hereafter heaven must be full of laughter!

UNKNOWN

Choose Joy

Ever wonder how you can be perfectly happy one minute and upset the next? If joy is a choice, then ...e you have to make. . .continually. We are often ... ur emotions, which is why it's so important ... used, especially when you're having a tough day. Don't let frustration steal even sixty seconds from you. Instead, choose joy!

JANICE HANNA

Friends Make Life Worthwhile

To laugh a bit and joke a bit and grasp a friendly hand. . .
to tell one's secrets, hopes, and fears and share a friendly
smile; to have a friend and be a friend is what makes life
worthwhile.

UNKNOWN

More Joy

More holiness give me, more striving within;
More patience in suffering, more sorrow for sin;
More faith in my Savior, more sense of His care;
More joy in His service, more purpose in prayer.

PHILIP P. BLISS

An Endless Fountain

A thing of beauty. . .still will keep
A bower quiet for us, and a sleep
Full of sweet dreams and health
and quiet breathing. . .
An endless fountain of immortal drink,
Pouring unto us from the heaven's brink.

JOHN KEATS

The Glory of Friendship

The glory of friendship is not the outstretched hand
nor the kindly smile nor the joy of companionship;
it is the spirited inspiration that comes to one when
he discovers that someone else believes in him and is
willing to trust him with his friendship.

RALPH WALDO EMERSON

An Inviting Aroma

Have you ever noticed that we're naturally drawn to people who are fun to be around. . .people who radiate joy? They are like a garden of thornless roses: They put off a beautiful aroma and draw people quite naturally. If you want to win people to the Lord, then woo them with your kindness. Put off an inviting aroma.

Win them with your love.
Radiate joy!

JANICE HANNA

A New Day

Today a new sun rises for me; everything lives,
everything is animated, everything seems to speak to
me of my passion, everything invites me to cherish it.

ANNE DE L'ENCLOS

Beautiful and Good

It seems to me we can never give up longing and
wishing while we are alive. There are certain
things we feel to be beautiful and good,
and we must hunger for them.

GEORGE ELIOT

To Laugh and Pray

It is often just as sacred to laugh as it is to pray.

CHARLES R. SWINDOLL

Joy in Simple Things

A Prayer: Give me work to do; give me health;
give me joy in simple things. Give me an eye for
beauty, a tongue for truth, a heart that loves, a mind
that reasons, sympathy that understands.

UNKNOWN

God and Grace Go Together

Grace is no stationary thing, it is ever becoming.
It is flowing straight out of God's heart. Grace does
nothing but re-form and convey God. . . . God,
the ground of the soul, and grace go together.

MEISTER ECKHART

Happiest Moments

The happiest moments my heart knows are those
in which it is pouring forth its affections to a few
esteemed characters.

THOMAS JEFFERSON

Great Things

The LORD has done great things for us, and we are filled with joy.

PSALM 126:3 NIV

The Greater Part of Happiness

I have learned from experience that the greater part of
our happiness or misery depends on our dispositions
and not on our circumstances.

MARTHA WASHINGTON

The Oil of Joy

What do the words "oil of joy" (Isaiah 61:3 KJV) mean to you? Can you envision the Lord anointing you with that precious oil? Do you feel it running down over your head and down your cheeks? Oh, that we would always sense the joy of His anointing. That we would see ourselves as usable to the Kingdom. Today, as you enter your prayer time, allow the Lord to saturate you with His oil of joy.

JANICE HANNA

Thy Will Be Done

And joys and tears alike are sent
To give the soul fit nourishment.
As comes to me or cloud or sun,
Father! Thy will, not mine, be done.

SARAH FLOWER ADAMS

Give Me a Sense of Humor

Give me a sense of humor, Lord,
Give me the grace to see a joke,
To get some happiness from life
And to pass it on to other folk.

UNKNOWN

Genuine Friends

Genuine friends can enter into our celebration with as much or more enthusiasm as they would have if the fortuitous serendipity had happened to them.

LLOYD JOHN OGILVIE

Earth Is a Cloak to Heaven

Life is so full of meaning and purpose, so full of
beauty, beneath its covering, that you will find earth
but cloaks your heaven.

FRA GIOVANNI

Changing Patterns

The patterns God plans for our days are always
changing. . .rearranging. . .and each design is
unique. . .graced with His own special beauty.

UNKNOWN

God Continually Works for You

You're working to please God, but did you know He's also been working for you? Every day, when you get up, you can count on God's protection, guidance, and the work of His Spirit.

PAMELA MCQUADE

Paradise

Flowers are God's thoughts of beauty, taking form to gladden mortal gaze; bright gems of earth, in which, perchance, we see what Eden was—what Paradise may be!

WILLIAM WILBERFORCE

Have Confidence before God

Our hearts are not made happy by words alone.
We should seek a good and pure life, setting our minds
at rest and having confidence before God.

THOMAS À KEMPIS

Happiness Comes From. . .

Happiness comes from the capacity to feel
deeply, to enjoy simply, to think freely,
to risk life, to be needed.

STORM JAMESON

Unexpected Happiness

ess is something that comes into our lives
1 doors we don't even remember leaving

ROSE WILDER LANE

Hugs

Everyone was meant to share God's all-abiding love
and care; He saw that we would need to know a way to
let these feelings show. . .so God made hugs.

JILL WOLF

Feeling Good

Laughter is the sensation of feeling good all over and showing it principally in one place.

JOSH BILLINGS

Few Things

As we grow, the time between good bouts of
fun and laughter grow, too. But its value remains
immeasurable—because there are few things in
life as important as joy, friends,
and the sound of laughter.

BONNIE JENSEN

Sing!

May none of God's wonderful works keep silence night or morning. Bright stars, high mountains, the depths of the seas, sources of rushing rivers: May all these break into song as we sing to the Father.

UNKNOWN

Fits of Laughter

We occasionally have moments when we're perfectly content to feel gloomy. . . .Then along comes a friend who manages to encourage a smile and can even send you into a fit of laughter.

ANITA WIEGAND

Needed Armor

A sense of humor is needed armor. Joy in one's lips is a sign that the person down deep has a pretty good grasp of life.

HUGH SIDEY

With a Merry Heart

Ever feel like nothing you do is good enough?
Your boss is frustrated over something you've
done wrong. The kids are complaining.
Your neighbors are even upset with you.
How wonderful to read that God accepts our
works, even when we feel lacking. He encourages
us to go our way with a merry heart, completely
confident that we are accepted in the Beloved.

JANICE HANNA

Shouts of Joy

[God] will yet fill your mouth with laughter and
your lips with shouts of joy.

JOB 8:21 NIV

Where Your Happiness Lies

Where your pleasure is, there is your treasure;
where your treasure, there your heart; where your
heart, there your happiness.

AUGUSTINE OF HIPPO

With the Heart

The best and most beautiful things in the world cannot be seen or even touched. They must be felt with the heart.

HELEN KELLER

May God Fill Your Heart

May the hand of a friend always be near you;
may God fill your heart with
gladness to cheer you.

IRISH BLESSING

Meditate on God's Word

You may look with awe at the perfection of the stars on a dark, clear night, and melt in joy at the sight of a newborn's perfect eyes, ears, fingers, and toes. With the same sense of wonder, consider God's commandments, spoken by God for your daily guidance and eternal good. He sets His commandments before you this day, inviting you to meditate on the boundless perfection of His words and take them, in their entirety, into your heart.

PATRICIA MITCHELL AND
REBECCA CURRINGTON

Strength

Do not pray for easy lives. Pray to be stronger. Do not pray for tasks equal to your powers. Pray for powers equal to your tasks.

PHILLIPS BROOKS

God Made All Things

All things bright and beautiful,
All creatures great and small,
All things wise and wonderful,
the Lord God made them all.

CECIL FRANCES ALEXANDER

The Cheerful Soul

The true source of cheerfulness is benevolence.
The soul that perpetually overflows with
kindness and sympathy will always be cheerful.

PARKE GODWIN

Pure Delight

Rejoicing in God? Those who do not know Jesus cannot imagine it. You have to know Jesus to delight in His presence, just as you cannot enjoy a friend until you come to know each other and enjoy companionship. But knowing and loving God brings us, His children, joy in His presence and the prospect of undefined pleasures at His side. Are you prepared to share those joys with Jesus for eternity?

PAMELA MCQUADE

In God's Hands

I have held many things in my hands, and I have lost them all; but whatever I have placed in God's hands, that I still possess.

MARTIN LUTHER

Laugh Always

I have always felt that laughter in the face of reality is probably the finest sound there is and will last until the day when the game is called on account of darkness. In this world, a good time to laugh is any time you can.

LINDA ELLERBEE

Wonderful Mystery

That I am here is a wonderful mystery to
which I will respond with joy.

UNKNOWN

Love Is an Image of God

Love is an image of God, and not a lifeless image,
but the living essence of the divine nature which
beams full of all goodness.

MARTIN LUTHER

Seek Goodness

Seek goodness in others. Love more persons more. . .
unselfishly, without thought of return. The return,
never fear, will take care of itself.

HENRY DRUMMOND

God's Spirit

If you want your neighbor to see what God's Spirit will do for him, let him see what it has done for you.

HENRY WARD BEECHER

Your Heart's Desire

There are many things in life that will catch your
eye, but only a few will catch your heart. . .
pursue those.

MICHAEL NOLAN

Perfect Miracle

To me, every hour of the day and night is an
unspeakable perfect miracle.

WALT WHITMAN

Life Is an Adventure

One way to get the most out of life is to look upon it as an adventure.

WILLIAM FEATHER

Beautiful and Unique

Some people weave burlap into the fabric of our lives,
and some weave gold thread. Both contribute to make
the whole picture beautiful and unique.

UNKNOWN

Endurance

Endurance in faith, hard as it may seem, brings happiness. Trials are not a sign of God's disfavor or His will to carelessly punish His children. The tenderhearted Savior never acts cruelly. But through troubles, we draw close to Him and see God's power at work in our lives. Then, like Job, when we persevere in faith, God rewards us bountifully.

PAMELA MCQUADE

Celebrate!

Celebrate and be glad forever! I am creating a
Jerusalem, full of happy people.

ISAIAH 65:18 CEV

Joyous Petitions

What are the deepest desires of your heart? Ponder that question a moment. If you could really do— or have—what you longed for, what would that be? The key to receiving from the Lord is delighting in Him. Draw near. Spend time with your head against His shoulder, feeling His heartbeat. Ask that your desires come into alignment with His will. Then, with utmost joy, make your petitions known.

JANICE HANNA

What Gives You Joy

We should all do what, in the long run, gives us joy,
even if it is only picking grapes or sorting the laundry.

E. B. WHITE

On the Good Side

Nothing contributes more to cheerfulness than
the habit of looking at the good side of things.

WILLIAM B. ULLATHORNE

What Makes Life Rich

Every day is a brand-new opportunity to offer our
hands, our hearts, our time, and our resources. . . .
It is the giving of ourselves that makes life rich.

BONNIE JENSEN

True Joy

This is the true joy in life, the being used for a purpose recognized by yourself as a mighty one.

GEORGE BERNARD SHAW

Full of Surprises

Humor is a spontaneous, wonderful bit of an outburst that just comes. It's unbridled, it's unplanned, it's full of surprises.

ERMA BOMBECK

Do the Best You Can

When we do the best we can, we never know
what miracle is wrought in our life or
in the life of another.

HELEN KELLER

Be Thankful

If you can eat today, enjoy the sunlight today, mix good cheer with friends today, enjoy it and bless God for it.

HENRY WARD BEECHER

Joy Is Straight Ahead

Trials have a purpose in our lives. As a smith heats up gold to purify it, God heats up our lives to make spiritual impurities rise to the surface. If we cooperate with Him, sin is skimmed off our lives, purifying our faith. Cleansed lives bring glory to God and joy to us. If a trial lies before you today, envision the joy ahead.

PAMELA MCQUADE

Keep Your Eyes on God

Keep your face upturned to Him as the flowers do the
sun. Look, and your soul shall love and grow.

HANNAH WHITALL SMITH

A Whole Life

The private and personal blessings we enjoy...
deserve the thanksgiving of a whole life.

JEREMY TAYLOR

You Are Part of the Great Plan

You are part of the great plan, an indispensable part.
You are needed; you have your own unique share in
the freedom of Creation.

MADELEINE L'ENGLE

Full of Peace and Joy

Where the soul is full of peace and joy, outward surroundings and circumstances are of comparatively little account.

HANNAH WHITALL SMITH

Don't Lose Sight

Let us not hurry so in our pace of living that we lose sight of the art of living.

SIR FRANCIS BACON

Abandon Yourself to God

Peace of consciousness, liberty of heart, the sweetness of abandoning ourselves in the hands of God, the joy of always seeing the light grow in our hearts, finally, freedom from the fears of insatiable desires of the times, multiply a hundredfold the happiness which the true children of God possess.

FRANÇOIS FÉNELON

The World Is a Looking Glass

The world is a looking glass and gives back to every man the reflection of his own face. Frown at it, and it in turn will look sourly at you; laugh at it, and with it, and it is a jolly, kind companion.

WILLIAM THACKERAY

Forever and Always

God doesn't change His mind. When He says He loves
us. . .He means it. He loves—forever and always!
And there's nothing you can do to change that. Nothing!

UNKNOWN

Enjoy Happiness

There is nothing better than to be happy and enjoy ourselves as long as we can.

ECCLESIASTES 3:12 NLT

Showers of Joy

Flowers are lovely; love is flower-like;
Friendship is a sheltering tree;
Oh, the joys that come down shower-like!

SAMUEL TAYLOR COLERIDGE

His Blessings

Every day God freely displays His blessings. Are we too busy or disinterested to appreciate their wonder? Even if we've forgotten He's there, reminders are all around for He is the God of covenants. In a world where promises (or covenants) are disregarded routinely, I need God's kind of stability.

CAROL L. FITZPATRICK

Rainbow Colors

God offers us His Spirit, not just as an encouragement, but as a heart changer. He enters into us and begins to redesign our interior life. Suddenly our actions and our words are truthful, kind, and fair. No longer do they reflect the blackness that painted our hearts, but the rainbow colors of His blessings.

PAMELA MCQUADE

A Bouquet of Happiness

Plant a seed of friendship; reap a bouquet of
happiness.

LOIS L. KAUFMAN

Happiness Is a Butterfly

Happiness is a butterfly, which, when pursued, is
always just beyond your grasp, but which, if you
will sit down quietly, may alight upon you.

NATHANIEL HAWTHORNE

Something Happy

For new, and new, and ever new,
The golden bud within the blue;
And every morning seems to say:
"There's something happy on the way."

HENRY VAN DYKE

Genuine Joy

If you have placed your hope and faith in God,
you have every reason to be happy. You know who you
are and whose you are. You have set your heart on doing
His will, and you hold to His promises to protect and
preserve you in any situation you may face in life.
Take a moment to thank Him for bringing you into the
light of His love, and cultivate a
spirit of genuine joy.

PATRICIA MITCHELL
AND
REBECCA CURRINGTON

Mountaintops and Valleys

A friend will joyfully sing with you when you are on the mountaintop and silently walk beside you through the valley.

UNKNOWN

Continual Conversation

There is no mode of life in the world more pleasing and more full of delight than continual conversation with God.

BROTHER LAWRENCE

Little Things

Girlfriends remind us that the happiness of life is made up of little things—a smile, a hug, a moment of shared laughter.

UNKNOWN

Sweet Savor

Your prayers certainly don't have to be elaborate or polished. God does not judge your way with words. He knows your heart. He wants to hear from you. His Word says that your prayers rise up to heaven like incense from the earth. Remember to send a sweet savor His way daily.

CAROL L. FITZPATRICK

A Good Morning

It was only a glad "Good morning,"
As she passed along the way,
But it spread the morning's glory
Over the livelong day.

CHARLOTTE AUGUSTA PERRY

A Joyful Song

Through all eternity to Thee
A joyful song I'll raise;
For oh! eternity's too short
To utter all Thy praise.

JOSEPH ADDISON

Gentle Joy

Joy descends gently upon us like the evening dew,
and does not patter down like a hailstorm.

JEAN PAUL RICHTER

Day 272

God Thinks about You!

God rejoiced at your birth. You were fashioned exactly the way He wanted you. How incredible to comprehend that when you awake in the morning, God is already thinking about you!

CAROL L. FITZPATRICK

Share the Joy

Sometimes God goes overboard when it's time to make provision. He blesses us above and beyond what we could ask or think. He not only meets our needs. . . He throws in a bit of excess, just to watch us smile. If you're in a season of abundant provision, remember to share the joy! Pass on a portion of what He has given you. And praise Him! What an awesome God we serve!

JANICE HANNA

Joy in Troubles

Joy? To be faced with trials should cause us joy?
Hard to imagine, isn't it? But God calls us to joy
when unbelievers persecute us because of our
faith or when our situation is merely difficult.
It is a joy to Him that we have stood firm in faith,
and He calls us to share His delight. That doesn't
mean we seek out trials but that we face the
situation hand in hand with God. In trials,
our spiritual strength increases.

PAMELA MCQUADE

God Is Only a Prayer Away

Every man prays in his own language, and there is
no language that God does not understand.

DUKE ELLINGTON

Be Filled with Joy

Be full of joy in the Lord.

PHILIPPIANS 3:1 NCV

Everyday Joy

Is it really possible to have joy in your everyday life...
even when the kids are crying and the bills are piling up?
When you're overwhelmed with work or struggling with
emotional problems? Can you truly "rejoice and be glad"
in the midst of such trials? Of course you can! Joy is a
choice, and it's one the Lord hopes you'll make in every
situation. His joy will give you the strength you need to
make it through. So, rejoice, dear one. Rejoice!

JANICE HANNA

Let Me Be Content

Let me, if I may be, ever welcomed to my room
in winter by a glowing hearth, in summer by a
vase of flowers; if I may not, let me think how
nice they would be and bury myself in my work.
I do not think that the road to contentment
lies in despising what we have not got. Let us
acknowledge all good, all delight that the world
holds and be content.

GEORGE MACDONALD

All Good Things Come from God

All that is good, all that is true, all that is beautiful, all that is beneficent, be it great or small, be it perfect or fragmentary, natural as well as supernatural, moral as well as material, comes from God.

JOHN NEWMAN

Joyful Expectancy

Cheerfulness brings sunshine to the soul and drives away the shadows of anxiety. To be cheerful under all circumstances is to radiate faith. It is an expression of hope and an attitude of joyful expectancy. . .it is to know that God holds all things in His control and that He neither slumbers nor sleeps.

HANNAH WHITALL SMITH

Give Thanks and Praise to God

It is right and good that we, for all things, at all times,
and in all places, give thanks and praise to You,
O God. We worship You, we confess to You,
we praise You, we bless You, we sing to You,
and we give thanks to You.

LANCELOT ANDREWES

Beauty of His Peace

Drop Thy still dews of quietness till all our
strivings cease; Take from our souls the strain
and stress, and let Our ordered lives
confess the beauty of Thy peace.

JOHN GREENLEAF WHITTIER

Without Fear

We walk without fear, full of hope and courage and strength to do His will, waiting for the endless good which He is always giving as fast as He can get us able to take it in.

GEORGE MACDONALD

Let Us Not Forget

The sun. . .in its full glory, either at rising or setting—
this, and many other blessings we enjoy daily;
and for the most of them, because they are so common,
most men forget to pay their praises. But let us not.

IZAAK WALTON

Unending Praise

May your life become one of glad and unending praise
to the Lord as you journey through this world, and in
the world that is to come!

TERESA OF AVILA

Nature's Treasures

If we are children of God, we have a tremendous treasure in nature and will realize that it is holy and sacred. We will see God reaching out to us in every wind that blows, every sunrise and sunset, every cloud in the sky, every flower that blooms, and every leaf that fades.

OSWALD CHAMBERS

This Is My Father's World

This is my Father's world:
He shines in all that's fair;
In the rustling grass I hear Him pass;
He speaks to me everywhere.

MALTBIE D. BABCOCK

Something Charming

There's surely something charming in seeing the smallest thing done so thoroughly, as if to remind the careless that whatever is worth doing is worth doing well.

CHARLES DICKENS

Happiness in Old Age

When grace is joined with wrinkles, it is adorable.
There is an unspeakable dawn in happy old age.

VICTOR HUGO

Your Success

If the day and the night are such that you greet
them with joy, and life emits a fragrance like
flowers and sweet-scented herbs,
is more elastic, more starry,
more immortal——that is your success.

HENRY DAVID THOREAU

Teach Me to Praise You

O God, great and wonderful, who has created the
heavens, dwelling in the light and beauty of it;
who has made the earth, revealing Yourself in every
flower that opens; let not my eyes be blind to You,
neither my heart be dead, but teach me to praise You,
even as the lark, which offers her song at daybreak.

ISIDORE OF SEVILLE

Heaven's Beauty Overflows

The full woods overflow among the meadow's gold!
A bluebell wave has rolled,
   where crowded cowslips grow.
The drifting hawthorn snow brims over hill and wold.
The full woods overflow among the meadow's gold. . . .
Heaven's beauty crowds below,
         the full woods overflow!

MARY WEBB

Valley of Love

'Tis a gift to be simple, 'tis a gift to be free,
'Tis a gift to come down where we ought to be—
And when we find ourselves in the place just right,
'Twill be in the valley of love and delight.

SHAKER HYMN

Attitude of Worship

Evening after evening in the summer, I have
gone to see the white clover fall asleep in the
meadow.... Everywhere in the dusk, the white
clover leaves are sleeping in an
attitude of worship.

MARY WEBB

Restored Joy

When you restore your home, you return it to its prior state—its best possible condition. But is it possible to restore joy? Can you really get it back once lost? Of course you can! Joy is a choice and can be restored with a single decision. Decide today. Make up your mind. Get ready for the renovation to take place as you ask the Lord to restore the joy of your salvation.

JANICE HANNA

I Am His and He Is Mine

Birds with gladder songs o'erflow,
Flowers with deeper beauties shine,
Since I know, as now I know,
I am His, and He is mine.

GEORGE WADE ROBINSON

Give Thanks

Give thanks unto the LORD, call upon his name, make known his deeds among the people, Sing unto him, sing psalms unto him, talk ye of all his wondrous works.

I CHRONICLES 16:8–9 KJV

May God Hold You

May the road rise to meet you,
May the wind be always at your back,
May the sun shine warm upon your face,
May the rain fall soft upon your fields,
And, until we meet again,
May God hold you in the palm of His hand.

IRISH BLESSING

Eternal Calm

The peace of God is that eternal calm which lies far too deep down to be reached by any external trouble or disturbance.

ARTHUR T. PIERSON

Nothing Is So Sweet

I know nothing so pleasant as to sit there on a summer
afternoon, with the western sun flickering through the
great elder-tree...where flowers and flowering shrubs
are set as thick as grass in a field, a wilderness of
blossom, interwoven, intertwined, wreathy, garlandy,
profuse beyond all profusion.

MARY RUSSELL MITFORD

Heaven's Bliss

Prayer is
The world in tune,
A spirit-voice,
And vocal joys
Whose echo is heaven's bliss.

HENRY VAUGHAN

Blessings upon Blessings

God, who is love. . .simply cannot help but shed blessing on blessing upon us. We do not need to beg, for He simply cannot help it!

HANNAH WHITALL SMITH

Summer Afternoon

Summer afternoon—summer afternoon; to me those have always been the two most beautiful words in the English language.

HENRY JAMES

A Little Flower

"Just living is not enough," said the butterfly.
"One must have sunshine, freedom, and a little flower."

HANS CHRISTIAN ANDERSEN

Made Beautiful

As a countenance is made beautiful by the soul's shining through it, so the world is beautiful by the shining through it of God.

FRIEDRICH HEINRICH JACOBI

Fill It

Life itself cannot give you joy unless you really
will it. Life just gives you time and space—
it's up to you to fill it.

CHINESE PROVERB

Cheap Medicine

Always laugh when you can. It is cheap medicine.

LORD BYRON

DAY 308

Rejoicing Pleases God

It is pleasing to God whenever you rejoice or laugh
from the bottom of your heart.

MARTIN LUTHER

Finding Happiness

The art of being happy lies in the power of extracting
happiness from common things.

HENRY WARD BEECHER

Think upon God

When I think upon God, my heart is so full of joy
that the notes dance and leap from my pen.

JOSEPH HAYDN

The Greatest Treasure on Earth

After the friendship of God, a friend's affection is the greatest treasure here below.

UNKNOWN

Sleep in Peace

When you have. . .accomplished your daily task, go to sleep in peace. God is awake.

VICTOR HUGO

A Joyous Crown

We are so focused on the joys of this life that we sometimes forget the exquisite joys yet to come in the next. Enduring and overcoming temptation can bring us great satisfaction here on earth, but imagine the crown of life we're one day going to receive. Nothing can compare! Oh, the joy of eternal life. Oh, the thrill of that joyous crown.

JANICE HANNA

Laugh at Yourself

It is of immense importance to
learn to laugh at ourselves.

KATHERINE MANSFIELD

Lighten Someone's Burden

No one is useless in this world who lightens the
burdens of it for another.

CHARLES DICKENS

Faithful in Little Things

Be faithful in little things, for in them our strength lies.

MOTHER TERESA

Fruit of the Spirit

The fruit of the Spirit is love, joy, peace, patience, kindness, goodness, faithfulness, gentleness and self-control. Against such things there is no law.

GALATIANS 5:22–23 NIV

God's Answers

Keep praying, but be thankful that God's answers
are wiser than your prayers!

WILLIAM CULBERTSON

Teach Me

Teach me, Father to value each day, to live, to love, to laugh, to pray.

KATHI MILLS

To Love...

Life is to be fortified by many friendships. To love and be loved is the greatest happiness of existence.

SYDNEY SMITH

Angels

Friends are the angels who lift us to our feet when our
wings have trouble remembering how to fly.

UNKNOWN

The Song in Your Heart

A friend hears the song in my heart and sings it to me when my memory fails.

UNKNOWN

Wisdom. . .What Joy!

Imagine you've lost a priceless jewel—one passed down from your grandmother to your mother and then to you. You search everywhere, under every rock, in every closet. Still, you can't find it. Finally, in the least likely spot. . .you discover it! Joy floods your soul! Now imagine that "jewel" is wisdom. You've stumbled across it, and oh, what a treasure! Talk about a happy find!

JANICE HANNA

Share in Joy

All who would win joy must share it; happiness was born a twin.

LORD BYRON

Each Day Is a Gift

God puts each fresh morning, each new chance of life
into our hands a gift to see what we will do with it.

UNKNOWN

The Road to Happiness

Take time to be friendly—
it is the road to happiness.

UNKNOWN

Peace and Tranquility

Good humor is one of the preservatives of our peace and tranquility.

THOMAS JEFFERSON

Surprise Gifts

I cannot count the number of times I have been
strengthened by another woman's heartfelt hug,
appreciative note, surprise gift, or caring question.

DEE BRESTIN

Laughter Is Like Sunshine

Laughter is the sun that drives winter from the face.

VICTOR HUGO

Joy Is to Be Shared

Of no worldly good can the joy be perfect,
unless it is shared by a friend.

LATIN PROVERB

Smile!

Any day is sunny that is brightened by a smile.

UNKNOWN

Trust God with Tomorrow

Ever wish you could see into tomorrow? Wish you knew what was coming around the bend?

While we can't see into the future, we can prepare for it by trusting God to bring us His very best. And while our "literal" vision can't glimpse the unseen tomorrow, we can prepare for it by staying close to the Lord and spending time in His Word. Peace and joy come when we trust God with our future!

JANICE HANNA

Complete Surrender

If you surrender completely to the moments as they pass, you live more richly those moments.

ANNE MORROW LINDBERGH

Add Joy

Add to your joy by counting your blessings.

UNKNOWN

Mirth

Mirth is God's medicine. Everybody ought to bathe in it.

HENRY WARD BEECHER

Net of Love

Joy is the net of love by which you can catch souls.

MOTHER TERESA

Better with God

GOD, your God, will outdo himself in making things go well for you. . .Yes, GOD will start enjoying you again, making things go well for you just as he enjoyed doing it for your ancestors.

DEUTERONOMY 30:9 MSG

Never Stop Laughing

We don't stop laughing because we grow old;
we grow old because we stop laughing.

MICHAEL PRITCHARD

The Simple Things in Life

I am beginning to learn that it is the sweet,
simple things of life which are the real ones after all.

LAURA INGALLS WILDER

Cheerfulness

Cheerfulness, like spring, opens all the blossoms of
the inward man.

JEAN PAUL RICHTER

Happiness Is Like Perfume

Happiness is a perfume you cannot pour on others
without getting a few drops on yourself.

RALPH WALDO EMERSON

Count It All Joy!

Temptations abound. We face them at every turn. On the television. In our conversations with friends. On the Internet. Today, as you contemplate the many temptations that life has to offer, count it all joy! The enemy knows we belong to the King of kings. That's the only reason he places stumbling blocks in our way. Next time he rears his ugly head, use joy as a weapon to fight him off.

JANICE HANNA

Today!

You can look ahead and obsess about fears for the
future or take life one day at a time and enjoy it.
But you only live in today, not in the weeks, months,
and years that may lie ahead. You can only change
life in the moment you're in now. Since worry never
improves the future and only hurts today,
you'll benefit most from trusting in God and enjoying
the spot where He's planted you for now.

PAMELA MCQUADE

Don't Cry over Spilled Milk!

If you can't make it better, you can laugh at it.

ERMA BOMBECK

Unexpected Sparks

Our brightest blazes of gladness are commonly
kindled by unexpected sparks.

SAMUEL JOHNSON

A Marvelous Gift

Humor is one of God's most marvelous gifts.

SAM ERVIN

Laughter Brings Happiness

Laughter is the brush that sweeps away the
cobwebs of the heart.

MORT WALKER

The Surest Way to Happiness

The surest way to be happy is to seek happiness for others.

MARTIN LUTHER KING JR.

God Will Always Love You

The supreme happiness of life is the conviction that we are loved—loved for ourselves, or rather, in spite of ourselves.

VICTOR HUGO

Abundant Joy

Hold a hand that needs
you and discover abundant joy.

FLAVIA WEEDN

Secret to Happiness

To be able to find joy in another's joy, that is the secret of happiness.

GEORGE BERNANOS

Each Happiness

Each happiness of yesterday is a memory of tomorrow.

GEORGE WEBSTER DOUGLAS

Reap What You Spend

The happiest business in all the world is that of making friends, and he who gives in friendship's name shall reap what he has spent.

ANNE S. EATON

Grace

It is a comely fashion to be glad—
joy is the grace we say to God.

JEAN INGELOW

Light Your Candle

Unshared joy is an unlighted candle.

SPANISH PROVERB

The Full Value of Joy

To get the full value of joy you must have somebody to divide it with.

MARK TWAIN

Not Far

You never have to look far to find a reason to share happiness.

UNKNOWN

Every Day

Write it on your heart that every day
is the best day of the year.

RALPH WALDO EMERSON

I Wish You Joy

I wish you all the joy that you can wish.

SHAKESPEARE

More than Meets the Eye

In what seems ordinary and everyday, there is always
more than first meets the eye.

CHARLES CUMMINGS

Joy Leads the Way

We're instructed to come into the Lord's presence with a joy-filled heart. . .to praise our way into the throne room. Perhaps you're not a musician. You don't own an instrument and only sing in the shower. Don't let that keep you from approaching the altar with a song of praise on your lips. Today, let joy lead the way, and may your praises be glorious!

JANICE HANNA

There Is Joy Ahead!

So be truly glad. There is wonderful joy
ahead. . . . You love him even though you have
never seen him. Though you do not see him now,
you trust him; and you rejoice
with a glorious, inexpressible joy.

1 PETER 1:6, 8 NLT

The Power of Love

Love is the divine vitality that everywhere produces
and restores life. To each and every one of us, it gives
the power of working miracles if we will.

LYDIA MARIA CHILD

Spread Joy

Try to make at least one person happy every day, and then in ten years you may have made three thousand six hundred and fifty persons happy, or brightened a small town by your contribution to the fund of general enjoyment.

SYDNEY SMITH

Success

She has achieved success who has lived well,
laughed often, and loved much.

BESSIE ANDERSON STANLEY

NOTES